CPS-MORRILL ES

3 24571 0902290 9   597.87 KIN
The life cycle of a poison

W9-ABU-139

The Life Cycle of a POISON DART FROG

NATURE'S LIFE Cycles

By Anna Kingston

Gareth Stevens
Publishing

Please visit our Web site, www.garethstevens.com. For a free color catalog of all our high-quality books, call toll free 1-800-542-2595 or fax 1-877-542-2596.

Library of Congress Cataloging-in-Publication Data

Kingston, Anna.
  The life cycle of a poison dart frog / Anna Kingston.
      p. cm. – (Nature's life cycles)
  Includes index.
  ISBN 978-1-4339-4692-9 (pbk.)
  ISBN 978-1-4339-4693-6 (6-pack)
  ISBN 978-1-4339-4691-2 (library binding)
  1. Dendrobatidae—Life cycles—Juvenile literature. I. Title.
  QL668.E233K56 2011
  597.87'7156–dc22

                                    2010031281

First Edition

Published in 2011 by
Gareth Stevens Publishing
111 East 14th Street, Suite 349
New York, NY 10003

Copyright © 2011 Gareth Stevens Publishing

Designer: Daniel Hosek
Editor: Therese Shea

Photo credits: Cover, pp. 1, 5, 7, 9, 17, 19, 21 (newly hatched tadpole, adult) Shutterstock.com; pp. 11, 14–15, 21 (egg, tadpole in metamorphosis) Joel Sartore/National Geographic/Getty Images; p. 13 Geoff Brightling/Dorling Kindersley/Getty Images.

All rights reserved. No part of this book may be reproduced in any form without permission in writing from the publisher, except by a reviewer.

Printed in the United States of America

CPSIA compliance information: Batch #CW11GS: For further information contact Gareth Stevens, New York, New York at 1-800-542-2595.

Contents

Words in the glossary appear in **bold** type the first time they are used in the text.

Beautiful and Deadly

Poison dart frogs can be bright colors such as blue, yellow, red, and gold. Some poison dart frogs have beautiful spots or stripes. The bright coloring is a warning. Poison dart frogs have poison in their skin! Their coloring warns other animals to stay away from them.

Some Native American peoples, such as the Emberá Chocó of Colombia, put poison from the frogs on darts they use for hunting.

AWESOME ANIMAL!

Poison dart frogs are sometimes known as poison arrow frogs, dart-poison frogs, or just poison frogs.

In nature, bright coloring is often a sign that an animal is poisonous.

5

A Wonderfully Wet Home

Like all frogs, poison dart frogs are **amphibians**. They have **lungs** for breathing, just like people do. They have very thin skin, which they also use to breathe. A sticky liquid called **mucus** covers the skin. Frogs must keep their skin wet in order to breathe through it. The mucus helps. A wet home helps, too.

Most poison dart frogs live in rainforests where it's hot, rainy, and wet all year. These rainforests are found in Central America and South America.

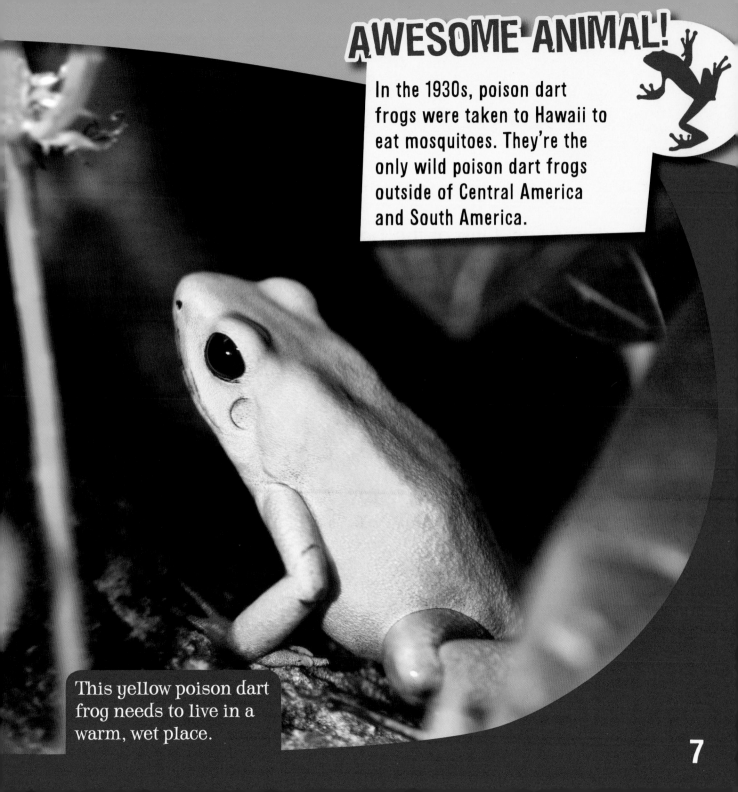

AWESOME ANIMAL!

In the 1930s, poison dart frogs were taken to Hawaii to eat mosquitoes. They're the only wild poison dart frogs outside of Central America and South America.

This yellow poison dart frog needs to live in a warm, wet place.

So Many Colors!

There are more than 100 **species** of poison dart frogs. One of the best known is the blue poison dart frog. It has bright blue skin with dark round spots. Strawberry poison dart frogs usually have bright red bodies and blue legs.

All poison dart frogs are small. Some are less than 1 inch (2.5 cm) long. The biggest are only about 3 inches (7.6 cm) long. All have strong back legs for jumping. They have pads on their toes that stick to things as they climb.

three-striped poison dart frog

yellow-banded poison dart frog

yellowback dyeing poison dart frog

green and black poison dart frog

Eggs

The life cycle of a poison dart frog starts when a male finds a **mate**. He calls a female with a loud chirping sound. When the female arrives, the frogs dance, bowing their heads. The female then lays her eggs, sometimes under a wet leaf. The male **fertilizes** the eggs.

Frog eggs are small and soft. They're covered in a special jelly to keep them safe. Over the next few weeks, one or both parents watch over the eggs.

This baby poison dart frog—called a tadpole—is inside its egg.

11

Tadpoles

When the eggs **hatch**, tadpoles come out. Tadpoles look like little fish. They even have **gills**. They move through water by wiggling their tails.

After hatching, poison dart frog tadpoles swim onto a parent's back. The parent carries the tadpoles to a watery place, such as a pond. Sometimes the tadpoles are taken to the water-filled leaves of plants called **bromeliads**. For a few weeks, parents of some species bring food to the tadpoles. Others leave the tadpoles to find their own food.

AWESOME ANIMAL!

Some poison dart frog mothers lay eggs that haven't been fertilized for their tadpoles to eat.

Can you see the tadpole in the water at the base of this bromeliad?

Adults

The tadpoles grow quickly. They go through a change in form. This change is called **metamorphosis** (meh-tuh-MOHR-fuh-suhs). The tadpoles begin growing legs. They lose their gills and breathe through their lungs. Finally, they lose their tails and become adult frogs.

Adult poison dart frogs spend most of their time near the rainforest floor. Some species, such as the blue poison dart frog, are good climbers.

AWESOME ANIMAL!

Once they become adults, it takes another year or more for poison dart frogs to mate.

In some poison dart frog species, the metamorphosis takes about 1 month. In other species, it can take up to 4 months.

Poison

Adult poison dart frogs spend part of their day looking for food. They eat small animals, such as **mites**, ants, crickets, termites, and beetles. They catch food with long, sticky tongues.

For many years, scientists wondered how poison dart frogs got their poisons. They knew the poisons came from body parts called glands. They noticed that poison dart frogs stopped being poisonous if they were taken out of the rainforest. They figured out that the frogs take in poisons from the food they eat.

The golden poison dart frog is the most poisonous of all. One frog has enough poison to kill 10 adults!

Poison dart frogs mostly eat small insects. Some eat animals larger than themselves.

An Unsafe World

Poison dart frogs are popular pets. However, people took so many wild frogs to sell as pets that soon there weren't many left in the rainforest! Today, laws keep too many poison dart frogs from being taken from the wild.

Poison dart frogs also face another danger. Large areas of rainforest are being cut down every day. Some of these frogs live in only one small part of the rainforest. If their homes are destroyed, the frogs will disappear.

AWESOME ANIMAL!

Rough-skinned poison dart frogs live only in one small forest in Costa Rica.

The future of poison dart frogs depends on people's actions.

Save the Frogs!

Frogs have thin skins. They can be hurt by changes in the air around them. Pollution causes problems for many frogs, including poison dart frogs.

Not all the news about poison dart frogs is bad. People around the world are putting aside land for wild animals, including poison dart frogs. Saving these frogs may help people, too. It may sound strange, but scientists are hoping to use the frogs' poisons to make **medicines**! Who knows what else we might learn from these amazing frogs?

The Life Cycle of a Poison Dart Frog

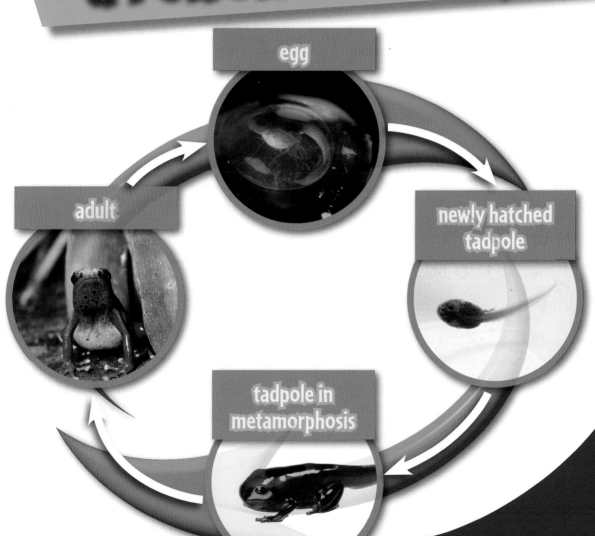

egg

newly hatched tadpole

tadpole in metamorphosis

adult

Glossary

amphibian: an animal that spends time on land but has babies and grows into an adult in water

bromeliad: a plant that stores water at the base of its leaves

fertilize: to add male cells to a female's eggs to make babies

gill: a body part that fish and other water animals use for breathing

hatch: to come out of an egg

lung: a body part that land animals use to breathe

mate: one of two animals that come together to make babies

medicine: something used to fight illness

metamorphosis: a complete change in form

mite: a tiny, eight-legged animal

mucus: a thick slime produced by the body of an animal

species: a kind of living thing. All people are one species.

For More Information

Books

Bredeson, Carmen. *Poison Dart Frogs Up Close*. Berkeley Heights, NJ: Enslow Publishers, 2009.

Dussling, Jennifer. *Deadly Poison Dart Frogs*. New York, NY: Bearport Publishing, 2009.

Wechsler, Doug. *Poison Dart Frogs*. New York, NY: Rosen Publishing Group, 2006.

Web Sites

Dart Poison Frog Vivarium
www.amnh.org/exhibitions/frogs/vivarium/
Read about the different colorful creatures called poison dart frogs.

Poison Dart Frogs
kids.nationalgeographic.com/kids/animals/creaturefeature/
poison-dart-frog/
Watch a video of a strawberry poison dart frog caring for her young.

Publisher's note to educators and parents: Our editors have carefully reviewed these Web sites to ensure that they are suitable for students. Many Web sites change frequently, however, and we cannot guarantee that a site's future contents will continue to meet our high standards of quality and educational value. Be advised that students should be closely supervised whenever they access the Internet.

Index